WALKS WITH CHILDREN
IN THE
YORKSHIRE DALES:

SWALEDALE and
WENSLEYDALE

WALKS with CHILDREN
in the Yorkshire Dales
SWALEDALE AND WENSLEYDALE

MARY WELSH

A Questa Guide

© Mary Welsh 1995
ISBN 1 898808 11 2

Questa Publishing
27 Camwood, Clayton Green, Bamber Bridge
PRESTON, Lancashire, PR5 8LA

ADVICE TO READERS

Readers are advised that while the author has taken every effort to ensure the accuracy of this guidebook, and has been required to revisit all the routes during the course of preparing the book, changes can occur which may affect the contents. The publishers would welcome notes of any changes that they find.

This guidebook has been compiled in accordance with the *Guidelines for Writers of Path Guides* published by the Outdoor Writers' Guild.

Printed by
Carnmor Print and Design, London Road, Preston

CONTENTS

SWALEDALE AND WENSLEYDALE

For young people, walking through Wensleydale and Swaledale for the first time is spellbinding. It is a region to which you can always return and recapture that first wonderful feeling. These two lovely dales are part of the Yorkshire Dales National Park, and have many footpaths, through glorious hay meadows and deciduous woodland. Tracks lead you over wild austere moorland, the haunt of curlew, dotterel, golden plover, snipe and skylark. There are steep climbs in both dales to please the more adventurous, and gentle strolls beside the Ure and the Swale for those seeking quietness and beauty.

Wensleydale is full of contrasts. Towards Leyburn the valley bottom spreads wide. Meadows are larger and there are fine trees creating an air of gracious parkland. Nearer the head of the dale, the limestone hills provide a wonderful foil for the bright green fields but do not overshadow them. Cotter End, Wether Fell, Addleborough and Penhill stand back, stepped and terraced, overlooking the River Ure. Towards Aysgarth it continues its journey by descending in dramatic waterfalls. Its tributaries, Cotter, Widdale, Hardraw, Gayle, Bain and Apedale, drop down in great exuberance to join the Ure.

It is a dale full of history. At Bainbridge it has a Roman road and a fort; near Carperby, West Burton and Castle Bolton are pre-Conquest and medieval lynchets, grassy terraces once ploughed by oxen; Middleham has motte and bailey earthworks, predating the remains of its castle; Bolton Castle, started in 1379, dominates the land around, and was Mary Queen of Scots' prison; the ruins of Jervaulx and Coverham abbeys are havens of peace; Nappa Hall is a fortified manor house, the battlemented towers of which provided protection in the turbulent 15th-century; Countersett was a focal point for Quakers.

Wensleydale has fine churches to visit. It has many villages with a wealth of gracious houses, cottages and other small dwellings grouped round a central green, where in the past cattle could be coralled at night for safety. Other villages are built on a linear plan, with the green towards one end. In 1202 Wensley was granted its market charter. It became very important and gave its name to the dale. But in the 16th-century it was devastated by the plague and its trade went to Leyburn, set on a hill with shops all round its spacious square. Delightful, too, is the market town of the upper dale, Hawes, a bustling cheerful place from which roads radiate in all directions.

An important industry in the dale was lead mining, and villages, like Preston-under-Scar, were built to house miners. Close by was Keld Head mine and Cobscar mine, which were dug into a lead-yielding belt of land that stretched across Wensleydale and into Swaledale.

Swaledale also retains much evidence of its mining past. Look for adits, huge flues, ruined buildings that once were smelt mills or peat stores, spoil heaps and hushes. Here, too, villages sprang up to house the miners - Healaugh, Gunnerside, Muker and Reeth are good examples. In the upper dale, memorials to the past are found in the ruins of mine buildings and the shattered rock of old quarry workings, not in great houses and abbeys.

Entering Swaledale from its western end is like stepping back in time. One narrow road, the B6270, traverses the narrow valley bottom, through which the River Swale (meaning swift) flows. It is hedged in by steep-sided, desolate fells, topped by broad lonely moors. Near Keld is the dramatic Kisdon Gorge where, in glacial times, the river changed its course, isolating Kisdon Hill. Then the valley widens a little, allowing for walled meadows in which stand the characteristic field barns.

Sheep farming is the main occupation of the scattered communities, and the breed of sheep is named after the dale and pronounced 'Swa'dle'. The likeness of a Swaledale ram appears on the emblem of the National Park.

The Swale continues on its tempestuous way, tumbling in numerous spectacular waterfalls. It is joined by many equally lively side streams, the Whitsundale Beck, East Gill, East Grain, Thwaite, Oxnop, Gunnerside and Barney. By the time the river reaches Grinton, joined by the Arkle, the valley has widened. The river, still fast flowing, passes through rich meadowland and past extensive lynchets.

At the entrance to the dale stands its capital, the fine town of Richmond, with its huge keep towering over a charming square and narrow alleys, known as wynds. Just outside the town's old wall lived the Grey Friars, and a beautiful tower of their monastery still stands. To the east of the town is Easby Abbey, where a branch of the Augustinian order enclosed land and bred sheep on a large scale. In the Middle Ages, much of Swaledale was controlled by monasteries, which attained great wealth from wool and lead. The lead was used by abbeys and castles throughout Britain and France for roofing and gutters. To the west of Richmond, Marrick Priory housed nuns, who wore black habits.

John Wesley came to Swaledale in the middle of the 18th-century. He preached to the miners, who appreciated a man they could understand. Many Methodist chapels were built, the money and often the labour coming from the miners themselves. They had a great wish to improve their education, as is shown by the existence of literary institutes at Muker, Gunnerside and Reeth.

The footpaths that criss-cross the two dales make for ideal walking. Start with the shorter walks and gradually work up to the more demanding ones when youngsters, for whom this book is compiled, are ready to tackle them. All the walks have interesting places to visit and young people will spot even more than are mentioned here. The views are magnificent. The wildlife reflects the soil and rock below. History, tragedy and comedy seem all about the dales. A gentle introduction to hill walking in such a glorious area will set children off on what could become a compulsive, lifelong and extremely healthy pastime.

WALK 1:
RAVENSEAT AND THE SOURCE OF THE SWALE

This challenging walk of contrasts should be attempted when you are sure youngsters are ready for an arduous seven to eight mile walk. It starts easily and then continues over stern, austere moorland. One of its aims is to see the source of the Swale, where the Birkdale and Great Sleddale Becks join. It is a walk for a good day, preferably after rain, because this is one of Swaledale's magnificent waterfall walks.

Start: Lower end of Keld village. Do not obstruct farm access or gateways. GR.893013.
Total distance: 12km (7½ miles).
Height gain: 129m (423 feet).
Difficulty: Easy walking. Moorland can be wet. Take care with young children if you return along the road, which can be busy in summer.

THE WALK:
Leave the lower end of Keld village by a track, Keld Lane, signposted Muker. Turn left at the Pennine Way sign to drop down the hedged way to the footbridge over the Swale. Ahead, East Gill Force descends in three turbulent falls - a foretaste of what is to come. Above the falls the Northern Coast to Coast Walk and the Pennine Way come together. Here turn left and take the track to East Stonesdale farm. Beyond the farmhouse, bear left to leave the Pennine Way, which continues to Tan Hill.

Take the good track, a bridleway that runs high above the river valley, with extensive views into the upper dale.

Below you can glimpse first Catrake Force and then Rainby Force, both petulant, foaming white and streaked with a rich brown peat stain as the river rolls over the rocky drops in its bed.

Descend to the footbridge over Stonesdale Beck, where

another fall races headlong.

Follow the continuing track to a gate and walk left to the hairpin bend. Take the stepped stile on the right and follow the signpost for Ravenseat. Ascend the path to walk the stiled way, west, along Cotterby Scar, a long escarpment of limestone cliffs, which support birch, ash, holly, yew and hawthorn. Below you can just see the famous Wain Wath Force. Continue on to pass below a fine avenue of beech. Ignore Low Bridge and go along a waymarked track, taking the upper track where it divides. Keep to the right of a farm and then on to pass the empty farm of Smithy Holme. Pass a Land Rover without wheels and follow a path over the moorland. Head for a post, with the sign Ravenseat/Keld, on the brow of slightly higher ground.

Stride on along the way, which is indicated by blobs of yellow paint on gates and barns. Take care as you peep over the wall on the left to view Oven Mouth and How Edge. In these dramatic ravines you can see the Whitsundale Beck make two sharp kinks to negotiate harder rock.

Stroll down the wild slopes, past two more waterfalls, to go through two gated stiles into Ravenseat.

This tiny hamlet was once a small thriving community of miners who earned their living in the coal seams on Tan Hill.

Turn left to cross a tractor bridge and then a packhorse bridge, which is possibly 18th-century and has been restored recently by the National Park. Stride the road out of the hamlet, climbing steadily to Hill Top and then on to join the B6270, where you turn right. Two hundred yards along look down left to see where the two becks join and the Swale comes into being.

Return along the B-road and drop downhill below Scots pine to cross High Bridge.

Beyond is another pleasing fall, and just beyond that the confluence of Whitsundale Beck with the Swale, where there is yet another lively fall. At Low Bridge, look for the well-preserved limekiln on the far side of the river.

If the road is busy you may wish to cross the bridge and turn left to take again your outward route above Cotterby Scar. If you continue along the road you have a good view of the lovely perpendicular limestone cliffs and, where Blackburn Beck joins the Swale, Wain Wath Force. From here it is a quarter-of-a-mile to Keld, or you may wish to cross Park Bridge and return by your outward route.

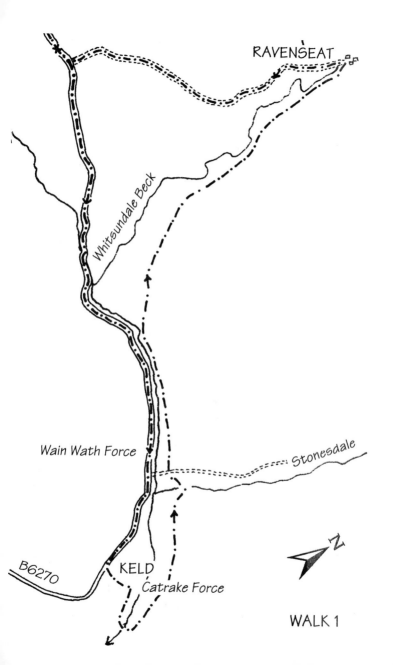

RAVENSEAT

Whitsundale Beck

Wain Wath Force

Stonesdale

B6270

KELD

Catrake Force

N

WALK 1

WALK 2:
MUKER TO KELD

Meadows, pastures and an ancient wood lie between the villages of Muker and Keld. You pass through these and beside the wide, swift-flowing River Swale, continuing along a high level moorland path that leads into a quiet lead-mining gill, once full of noise and bustle. The return to Muker is on wide grassy flats beside the stately river. The walk is full of interest for young and old alike, but both should exercise care by the river and in the gill.

Start: Car park at the east end of Muker. GR.912978.
Total distance: 11½km (7 miles).
Height gain: 330m (1083 feet).
Difficulty: Easy walking along the banks of the River Swale. If Kisdon Force is visited it needs to be approached with care. On the return path through Swinner Gill walkers need a head for heights for a short distance.

THE WALK:

Leave the car park and walk west (left), through the attractive village of Muker, passing in front of the magnificent literary institute. Turn right and then left to pass behind the Post Office. Follow the signpost directing you left which stands in the far left corner of the short road. Walk the reinforced track, passing to the right of the Old Vicarage and to the left of a house named Breconside. Where the track swings sharp left, stride ahead to a metal gate in the wall corner. It gives access to a track, initially muddy, but soon a pleasure to walk, with the valley of the Swale unfolding ahead.

Pass through three gates and then stride a wide grassy track, dropping down to a barn with a footpath sign to Keld. Walk over the pastures, passing through four waymarked gaps or stiles. Look for a small wooden gate in the wall on the right that leads to the alder-lined riverside walk. Continue to the stile in the wall ahead and carry on along the stiled way where in summer you will see white-rumped wheatears flitting about the walls and rocky outcrops. Walk ahead along the waymarked path for nearly half-a-mile. Keep to the left of the wall as you continue.

If you look across the pasture on the right you can see the ruined farm of Hartlakes, known as Boggle House because of the ghosts believed to haunt it.

Stride on through the dale, much-favoured by goldfinches, willow warblers, thrushes and chaffinches. Continue along a short stretch of a sunken walled track and then on to a gate into the ancient woodland of Kisdon Force Wood. Continue on the steady uphill climb along the stony track. At a T-junction of paths you join the Pennine Way to walk onwards. Just beyond, a footpath sign on the right directs you to Kisdon Force, magnificent double falls set in a glorious wooded hollow.

Keep on along the Pennine Way. Where the trees end on the right, look right for the best view of the triple falls of East Gill. Ignore a right turn (where the Pennine Way crosses the Swale), and continue to the tiny village of Keld.

Here, in this highest village in

Swaledale, grey cottages built of fine, closely grained stone taken from local quarries, cluster round the literary institute, the old school and the imposing United Reform Church. A seat by the small green might be just the place for lunch.

Walk back along the track to join the Pennine Way, a stony tree-lined path, dropping left, to a gate and the bridge over the river. Go up the path, with East Gill Force to your right. Bear right, cross the bridge over the beck and walk east along the high level path.

This is part of the Northern Coast to Coast Walk and from it there are grand views over Kisdon Gorge to Kisdon Hill. Below lies Kisdon Force, heard but not seen. Where the track curves, look left to see the spoilheaps of the Beldi Hill lead mines.

Cross a small arched bridge and then take a grassy track off left. This winds uphill and passes above the ruins of Crackpot Hall, once the highest inhabited farmhouse in Yorkshire.

Walk on the good track past the old smithy and pass through the gate to continue towards the head of spectacular Swinner Gill. Look for the ruined Swinnergill smelting mill (1770-1821), an old mine entrance, and the lovely falls.

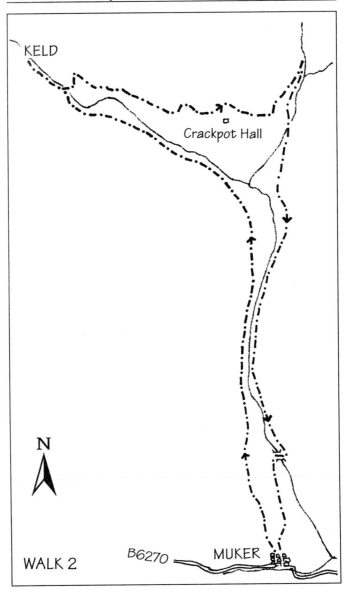

KELD

Crackpot Hall

N

WALK 2 B6270 MUKER

At the miners' bridge you can leave the right-of-way and clamber up the bed of the beck to see Swinnergill Kirk, a large cave with a narrow low entrance hidden behind a sheltering waterfall. It was used as a secret place of worship in the 17th-century. The 'kirk' should be visited only if there is little or no water in the mountain stream.

Return to the little bridge, climb the path descended earlier and leave it, left, after 200 yards. Follow, with utmost care, the narrow but exhilarating path that first runs high above the gill and then drops down to a narrow ford, which you cross. Stride up the slope to a stile and continue on high above the Beldi Smelt Mills (built 1771), in the gill. The path then leads down to join the wide cart track in the direction of Muker.

After 1½ miles, and many backward views of Kisdon and its gorge, take the right branch of the track that leads to Ramps Holme footbridge across the Swale. Beyond follow the well-signposted field path to return to Muker.

ALONG THE WAY:

Muker: is proud of the two naturalists Richard and Cherry Kearton. They walked to its school each day from the hamlet of Thwaite, where they were born in the 1860s. Muker at the time would have resounded to the feet of the men heading towards the lead mines. In the 1890s the brothers began to take their first photographs. Look for the memorial plaques to the brothers on the old school, now a craft shop.

Kisdon Hill: stands isolated high above its gorge through which flows the Swale. On its other side is a small stream and the road; it was not always so. Once the river flowed where now the small stream hurries by. Later, the waters of a melting glacier broke through the hillside east of Keld and the river found a new course.

Walls and barns: The walls of Swaledale were built to enclose grazing land. The field barns, one for two or three fields, were used to store hay and house cattle during the winter. The cows spent summer in the meadows, then in November were moved into the barns, four or five to each stall. Twice a day the farmer would visit all his barns to feed the cattle from the stored hay and to milk them. He would also remove the dung which dropped into a channel. Today the cattle are housed near the farm and the barns are rarely used.

WALK 3:
THWAITE TO ANGRAM VIA KISDON

Thwaite is a Norse name, meaning a clearing in woodland, but today little woodland surrounds the pleasing grey-brown village. Birches, alders and sycamores are scattered along the edge of becks, and copses clothe scar slopes. Around the village stretch small enclosed pastures, many with characteristic sturdy barns.

It is a delightful place from which to start a walk. The route follows the Pennine Way as far as Kisdon, half way up the hillside. It then crosses Kisdon Hill on a wonderful elevated grassy track, with rewarding views. The way back is along the valley bottom, damp in places, where the large number of stiles will provide a good challenge to youngsters to find the way.

Start: Large lay-by just before the nameplate for Thwaite at the bottom of the pass over Buttertubs. GR.893980.
Total distance: 7km (4½ miles).
Height gain: 190m (623 feet).
Difficulty: Easy walking generally. Exhilarating climb to hill top. Very rough track to join the B6270 at Thorns.

THE WALK:

From the lay-by descend to the village, crossing the sturdy bridge over the frolicking Thwaite Beck. Look upstream to see an attractive waterfall. In front of the Kearton Guest House, turn right.

Richard and Cherry Kearton, sons of a shepherd, were born in Thwaite and went to school in Muker. Richard wrote books on the countryside and Cherry photographed wildlife. They were pioneers of today's wildlife films. When they wished to get close to the animals they were filming, they wore sheepskins or rigged up flimsy but realistic hides.

Stride to the end of the lane to two signposts and a gap stile. Beyond, walk the narrow walled path to pass through two gap stiles and then turn sharp left to continue on the Pennine Way. Pass through a gate and cross to a tractor bridge over Skeb Skeugh. Bear right and then left uphill, beside a wall, to a signposted stile. Beyond, continue ascending on the clear path over the heather-covered slopes, with glorious extensive views of the dale below. Pause at the cairn to look across to Great Shunner Fell and the road over Buttertubs Pass.

Keep above Doctor Wood and press on the clear way, through a waymarked gate and on to a Pennine Way sign, directing you right to the back of Kisdon Farm. Carry on through two gates to walk a walled track, which passes a limekiln. At a three-armed signpost, leave the Pennine Way and continue climbing steadily along the bridleway to Keld. Go on up a walled way to a gate on to the open fell. Stride on with a wall to the right and, at the boundary ahead, turn left. From here you can see Swinner Gill, above the River Swale.

As you step out over the moorland top of Kisdon, think of the medieval mourners who carried the coffins of their loved ones in the opposite direction, because this is the old corpse road from Keld to Grinton.

Then begins a gentle descent, following the sign for Keld. The track, once cobbled, becomes very rough just before it reaches the valley bottom. Cross the ford by a clapper bridge and continue to the road, at Thorns, where you turn left.

A hundred yards along take an easy-to-miss stile on the left. Thirteen stiles are passed through as you walk the pastures to join the road again at Angram: as you go, keep above the field barns. Turn left along the road to take another signposted stile on the left. Another twelve stiles bring you to the walled track at Thwaite. On the way two small gills are crossed by a track or a footbridge. This last part of the walk comes close to the Skeb Skeugh and after rain can be wet, so pick your way carefully.

At the walled track, turn right to return.

ALONG THE WAY:
Meadows: Several paths radiate from Thwaite and these pass through hay meadows where you are asked to walk in single file. These meadows are farmed by traditional methods

and man-made fertilisers avoided. This results in a myriad of wild flowers. In mid-summer the fields are a mass of yellow buttercups, followed by cow parsley, sweet cicely and meadow cranesbill. Look also for the delicate but prolific mountain pansy.

Stiles: You cannot fail to notice the stiles on this walk - and on all walks in this book. Most are gap stiles, formed by two well-placed slabs of stone. Many have small gates where the gap widens towards the top. Some are stone-stepped. All do their job well, providing access through the walls and keeping stock out.

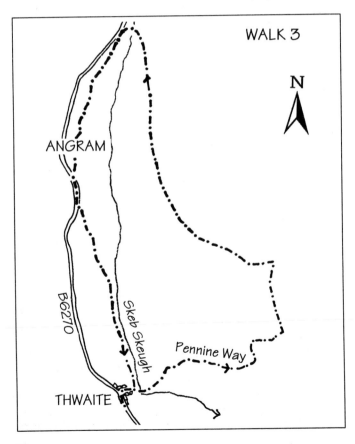

WALK 4:
GUNNERSIDE TO IVELET

The old road from Gunnerside towards Calvert Houses has been superseded by the B-road that runs through Swaledale. This walk from Gunnerside uses this old road, from where extensive views unfold. To reach the high-arched single-spanned packhorse bridge over the River Swale you pass through the hamlet of Ivelet, which stands on a limestone terrace. The return walk through the stiled pastures is pure joy and perhaps the one that youngsters will enjoy most.

Start: Parking area by bridge over beck, Gunnerside. GR.951983.
Total distance: 4km (2½ miles).
Height gain: 60m (197 feet).
Difficulty: Easy walking all the way. On one short stretch of path, overlooking the Swale, care should be taken.

THE WALK:

Leave Gunnerside by the road to the side of the Post Office, heading due west, to pass a small green. Continue on the high level way, which is almost vehicle-free. *The slopes of Gunnerside Pasture lie to your right and there is a pleasing view down towards the Swale, with its walled pastures about it.* Follow the road as it turns sharp left, crossing Grains Gill. Where it turns sharp right to continue, stride ahead.

Look right to see Gunnerside Lodge, at the time of writing the home of Lord Peel, the great-great-grandson of Sir Robert Peel, founder of the police force. Lord Peel is the owner of the 35,000 acre Gunnerside Estate, which through careful management of the grouse moors maintains the famous heather hillsides of the Yorkshire Dales National Park.

Descend the curving road to Ivelet. Carry on downhill along the alder-and ash-fringed road, beside an attractive stretch of the river, to see Ivelet Bridge. A large seat stands in this quiet corner, an ideal place for a picnic.

Return to the hamlet and take the signposted way, right, for Gunnerside. Follow the waymarked footpath, dropping to a footbridge over Shore Gill. Look upstream to see some delightful falls. From now on no directions are needed for the return through hay meadows. To the right, across the wide river, you can see the hamlet of Satron, shadowed by Lovely Seat. Just beyond the short unfenced section of the path is a stile to an easy path down to the side of the river, where everyone will want to dally.

ALONG THE WAY:

Ivelet Bridge: spans the Swale at a wide part of the river. Until the 19th-century ponies carried lead from local mines across the bridge. Look for the corpse stone on the far end of the parapet. Relays of bearers carried coffins in wicker baskets and laid them on the stone while resting. In 1580 a church was built at Muker but until then the bearers took two days to journey the 12 miles from Keld to consecrated ground at St Andrew's, Grinton. A legend says that a headless dog haunts the bridge and that bad luck comes to anyone who sees it.

While in Gunnerside, look for the fine Methodist chapel, built in 1789 and rebuilt in 1866. Methodism flourished in the dale, where in the 19th-century 2000 men and boys worked the lead mines around the village. A welcome but infrequent visitor was John Wesley.

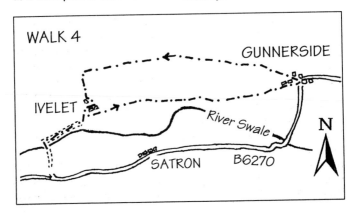

WALK 5:
GUNNERSIDE TO LOW ROW

From the high airy paths that run across the slopes you have dramatic views down into Swaledale. Here the river flows graciously, and in sunlight turns to a silver ribbon threading its way through the green pastures of the dale bottom. These pastures are joined by stone walls. Studding the slopes are sturdy barns, one to every two or three fields. Young people will enjoy the return walk, looking across the dale to see where they have walked earlier. There are many stiles to look for in the walls ahead and this gives youngsters the chance to develop their map reading skills by locating them.

Start: By the post office, Gunnerside. GR.951983.
Total distance: 7km (4½ miles).
Height gain: 50m (165 feet).
Difficulty: Easy.

THE WALK:

From the post office walk ahead to cross the Little Bridge over Gunnerside Beck. Continue past the small green and after the last house on the right take the gated reinforced track, left, up the slope. Just beyond a seat on the first zigzag, pursue the hedged track, climbing right. From the pleasingly stepped, and then grassy, way enjoy the views up and down the dale.

Step across Stanley Gill and stride ahead along the walled way towards Heights. Beyond the first house take a stepped stile in the wall on the right. Continue in front of two more houses and then carry on through four more gap stiles, with magnificent Swaledale at your feet. Keep to the right of a wall to follow a path through Rowleth Wood, which can be muddy after rain. Ash, yew and

21

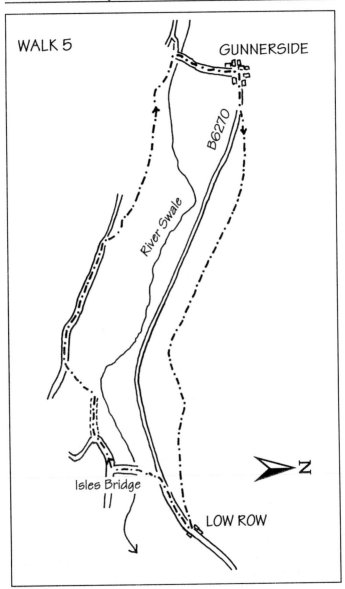

WALK 5

GUNNERSIDE

B6270

River Swale

Isles Bridge

LOW ROW

N

hazel grow about the slopes and through these slip many birds. Emerge from the wood and stroll on the stiled way to pass in front of the barn at Smarber Farm. Bear left, join a track, walk on to cross a lively beck by a footbridge and immediately bear right to pass through a gate to join a wide grassy track. Pass in front of Smarber Cottage and steadily descend. Continue to a footbridge over a dancing beck, which tumbles in three white-topped falls hidden in a leafy gill. Stride on to join the road at Low Row, a hamlet which sprawls along the hillside.

Turn right and walk along the narrow road to take the left turn for Crackpot. Cross Isles Bridge, with its many flood holes, over the Swale, and walk on to the T-junction, where you turn right.

Go on along the narrow lane to take a stone stepped stile on the left just past the last barn of Haverdale Farm. Climb straight uphill to the next stile and then strike diagonally right to the next to join the road by going diagonally across the next pasture.

Turn right and walk the lovely narrow lane to pass Bank Head cottages (1753). Take the diverted footpath, just beyond on the right. Drop down the slope and then take a lower terrace-like track along the dale side. From now on the stiled way continues roughly on the same contour. It passes to the right of the first barn and left of the second and through several gateless gaps. Join a track and continue to a small gate, on the right, that gives stepped access to the B6270. Turn right, cross Gunnerside New Bridge and walk on into the village.

ALONG THE WAY:

Limekilns: Throughout the Dales you come upon limekilns, set against a hillside. Inside is a shaft, tapering towards the top. At the bottom of the kiln, peat, wood and sometimes coal was used to ignite lumps of limestone. Workers loaded more limestone into the kiln from the top, reaching it by a ramp. The lime, after firing, was extracted from the base.

Burnt lime was needed as a fertiliser to reduce the acidity of soil, grazing animals needed its calcium, and it was also used, mixed with water and sand, in mortars and plasters for houses.

Lime-rich soils result in good grassland. Ash is the dominant tree, accompanied by yew, hazel, beech, lime, holly, pine, rowan, birch, hawthorn, hornbeam and blackthorn, many of the latter being found in Rowleth Wood. Oak, alder and sycamore grow nearer the valley bottom.

WALK 6:
REETH TO GRINTON

There is much of interest on this walk: a high moorland track with dramatic views into the upper dale; a delightful riverside stroll; three pleasing villages, one with a museum; Romano-British earthworks; Anglo-Saxon strip lynchets and a church with traces of Norman architecture.

Reeth, where the walk starts, is known as the small capital of Swaledale. Healaugh, half-way along, once housed dozens of lead miners in newly-built cottages. And where the walk nears its end at Grinton, you'll be in the parish that was once the largest in Yorkshire, stretching from near Richmond to Keld.

Start: Reeth village green. GR.038993.
Total distance: 9km (5½miles).
Height gain: 180km (688 feet).
Difficulty: Easy walking all the way.

THE WALK:

Reeth lies at the foot of Arkengarthdale. It was once the centre of a vast lead mining area. Today its many houses and shops stand peacefully around a spacious green. From it you can see the dale opening out, becoming more cultivated and wooded and you realise that upper Swaledale ends here.

Leave the green and turn left into Silver Street to walk in front of The Buck Hotel. Continue past the fire station and climb the hill. Just before the school at the top, take a narrow walled track on your right, signposted Skelgate Lane. Follow this steadily, climbing for more than half-a-mile, pausing on your way to enjoy views of the austere Fremington Edge and down into Reeth.

Pass through a gate on to the open moor and continue ahead

with the wall to your left. Stride on past Riddings Farm on your left and go on to walk beneath Calver Hill (420m) on your right. Here look for hares loping through the heather and grouse flying up, giving their characteristic call, which sounds like 'go back, go back'. Continue beside the dark gritstone wall and pause occasionally to peer over at the fascinating field patterns that quilt Harkerside on the far side of the valley. Look out for walled fields shaped like cups and jugs - no-one knows the reason!

Carry on along the good track to pass a cottage named Moorcock. Join a reinforced track which swings sharply left, and follow it as it drops steeply down to the village of Healaugh. Youngsters might wish to turn right here to see the interior of a very ordinary red phone box. You will be in for a surprise. To continue the walk, turn left to walk the narrow street, which is bordered by pretty cottages and houses.

Turn right beyond the last house, following a grassy track (signposted Grinton and Reeth), and stride on to the side of the alder-lined River Swale. Turn left and begin the lovely stiled walk beside the fast-flowing water to a suspension bridge, erected in 1921, which you cross.

Pause here and look across the river to see the cultivation terraces on the slopes below Reeth School. Turn left and walk along the riverbank and then, when the river makes a large meander, the continuing stiled way. Before you reach the side of the river again, look for traces of the earthwork running down the slopes, west of Dyke House Farm. Then look for the conical hill on the right, named a 'tumulus' (a burial site) on the OS map. Continue to a narrow lane where you turn left. Walk on to the tiny hamlet of Grinton, once a busy market town. *Here the dale ceases to be hard, austere and all stones, and becomes softer and well-wooded.*

You might like to visit the early Norman church of St Andrew's, known as the cathedral of the dale. It has a 'leper squint' and a copy of Birkett's new testament.

Continue through the hamlet to cross the Swale by the fine-arched bridge. Take the gated steps on the left to stride across a meadow. Look right beyond the first stile for more traces of the earthwork. Follow the way (yellow blobs on trees) to the side of the Arkle Beck. *On your right stands a house that was once a cornmill and later supplied electricity for the village; look for the mill race*

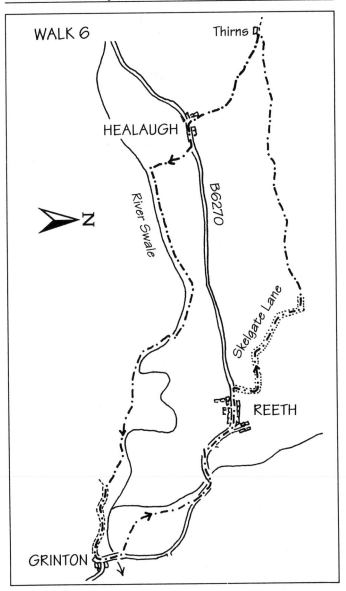

WALK 6

Thirns

HEALAUGH

River Swale

B6270

N

Skelgate Lane

REETH

GRINTON

covered with slabs. At the path end, join the road and turn left to cross another arched bridge and continue uphill towards the green. *Here make time to bear right up a cobbled lane to visit the Swaledale Folk Museum which depicts the past life styles of the people who inhabited the Dales. Displays include lead mining, farming, village life and traditions. (For further details telephone 01748 84373).*

ALONG THE WAY:

Lynchets: Strip lynchets look like long gigantic grassy steps. They were agricultural terraces,created by our Anglo-Saxon ancestors, for growing crops in the sixth and seventh centuries. Crops were grown on the strips between the ridges. Ploughing was carried out using teams of oxen pulling heavy wooden ploughs.

By the suspension bridge you can see the many small walled enclosures stretching up the hillsides, including the cup and jug fields referred to earlier. These extend to the riverside so that every owner had access to water and a share of the richer soil lower down.

Sheep: are undemanding animals which will nibble happily at thing pasture and graze it to the ground. They have to be hardy enough to withstand the cold and wet of winter.

Apart from the Herdwick, the Swaledale is the hardiest of all British sheep. It is identified by a fine set of spiral horns and a black face about a white nose. It has an important role as a crossing breed, the mother of such hybrids as the Mule and the Masham. Many of the great abbeys of Yorkshire grew rich from the wool clipped from their great flocks.

Swaledale: is part of the Yorkshire Dales National Park. The national park does not own the land and cannot make landowners do what the do not want to. It tries by education and advice to preserve the distinctive landscape made by generations of farmers, to preserve the scenery, the wildlife and the traditional buildings.

The national park does not promote tourism, but seeks to help visitors enjoy the dale. It repairs footpaths and stiles. Much of this work is seen on walks in this book.

WALK 7:
MARRICK TO HIGH FREMINGTON

Marrick is a quiet brownstone hamlet high on the slopes above the Swale. When the old road from Richmond passed through it to Reeth it was a much more important and busy place. Its chapel and church are now dwellinghouses. It has a small triangular green with a seat, and is reached by narrow roads over spacious rolling pastures, because this is the area where Swaledale begins to widen and its contours become softer.

Start: The viewing area at Reels Head. GR.064988.
Total distance: 7km (4½ miles).
Height gain: 159m (522 feet).
Difficulty: Easy walking all the way.

THE WALK:

Before you start from the wide verge parking area at Reels Head enjoy the magnificent view of Grinton and the dale beyond, then drop down the narrow lane towards the distant hamlet (west). Look right to see a well-preserved limekiln, and descend by ash woodland keeping a look out for long-tailed tits and goldfinches. Ignore the footpath on the left and continue to the bend in the road. Pass through the waymarked stile on the right, signposted Fremington. Proceed to the far left corner, with the bleak slopes of Fremington Edge towering to your right. Walk on, with the wall to the right, edging round the wall end on the left if the stile is blocked. Stride ahead along the stiled and gated way, with the now pleasingly wooded slopes of the Edge above. Cross a track and stride along a causeway to a metalled lane. Turn left and follow the lane as it winds steadily downhill, through the peaceful settlement of High Fremington. At the B6270 turn left and walk towards Grinton Bridge. Do not cross but descend the slope left to join a delightful

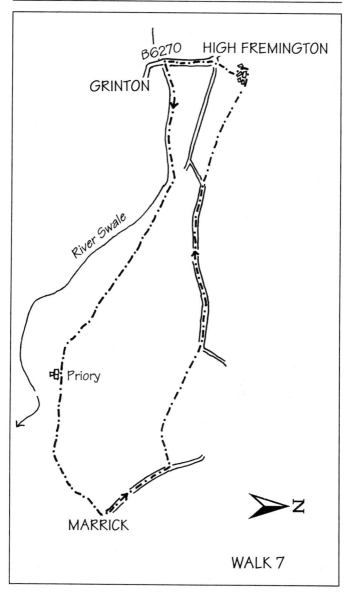

WALK 7

riverside path. Look across the surging Swale to see extensive Iron Age earthworks on the far bank. Keep to the path by the river until it joins the road, where you turn right. Stride on through the broad valley pastures that have replaced the fell slopes of the upper dale.

Then you come to Marrick Priory, a 12th-century house and a 13th-century tower, built for Benedictine nuns. It is now cared for by English Heritage, part of a working farm and also an outdoor centre. It is sited on a glorious stretch of the river, with pleasing woodland close by and meadows all around. It is a wonderful corner of Swaledale but perhaps you will find it difficult to reconcile the gaily coloured canoes and the computers of the centre with the gentle ruins.

Just past the Priory entrance take the signposted path on the left and climb into Steps Wood, following the splendid flagged way (known as The Nuns Causey) up through the glorious ash woodland. At the exit gate enjoy a splendid view down to the Swale. Continue ahead with the wall to your right and walk into the hamlet of Marrick.

At the T-junction turn left and continue uphill past the small green on your right and the farm on your left. Continue climbing and then descend to take a stile on your left before the first wall. Ascend beside it to a gated stile, pass through and walk up beside the wall, now on your left. Continue on the stiled way. From the top of the slope you can see the market stalls on the green at Reeth. Go on to a gate to the road and walk on to the viewing area at Reels Head.

ALONG THE WAY:

A story is told of Isabella Beaufort, who was courted by Henry VIII. She did not return his affection and sought sanctuary at Marrick Priory. The nuns kept her hidden for four years but allowed her to write to her sweetheart, Edward Herbert. When Henry dissolved the priories and monasteries the nuns had to go, but Isabella married Edward and they lived happily ever after in Somerset.

WALK 8:
RICHMOND TO APPLEGARTH

Attempt this when you are sure the children are ready for a longer walk. There is a steady, continuing climb all the way to Whitcliffe Scar. Then the path is sheer joy, with tremendous views ahead and in retrospect. Willance's Leap is a great place for a picnic but younger children will have to take care on the steep slopes. On return, leave time to explore the magical corners of Richmond, the capital of Swaledale.

Start: Nuns Close Car Park, Hurgill Road, Richmond. GR.168012.
Total distance: 10km (6½ miles).
Height gain: 180m (590 feet).
Difficulty: Steady climbing on the outward route but it is nearly all downhill on the return to Richmond.

THE WALK:

From the car park go downhill to Victoria Road and turn right. Pass the end of Quaker Lane and take a road called Westfields, which climbs right of West End Terrace post office and stores. The shop stands on the corner where the main road bends left. Begin the steady road climb, with superb views across Swaledale. There are several seats on the green terrace to the left where you might like to pause. Continue for nearly a mile (this is part of the Northern Coast to Coast Walk) to pass Whitcliffe Farm. Here you might see bullfinches in the hedgerows lining the lane.

Go on along the waymarked 'No Through Road' where the lane, now a reinforced track, narrows. Opposite High Leases Farm take the unmarked stile on the right. Beyond, walk straight up the slope to a marker post and enjoy the view of Sutton Bank, far beyond Richmond Castle.

Turn left and walk beside a derelict field boundary hedge to a gateless gap. Go through and stride on, with a fantastic view ahead, keeping parallel with the fenced Whitcliffe Wood to your left. Climb the two stiles at the junction of walls and bear left. Walk the stiled way, with a fence to the left, along the edge of Whitcliffe Scar. Look right to see Richmond Beacon on Beacon Hill. Go on along the magnificent ridge to a gate on the left, which gives access to the monument and stone erected in memory of Robert Willance of Richmond.

Sit here for your picnic and enjoy the view of Penhill, vast and flat-topped. Beyond look for Little and Great Whernside. To the west is a superb view into the upper dale and of the graciously curving River Swale.

Continue along the scar, now unfenced, where children should be well supervised. Go on past three huge limestone buttresses and carry on along beside the wall. At a small TV booster, follow the curving grassy way to the narrow tarmac road below, where you turn left. This is a delight to walk, with grassy slopes to the left and wooded slopes to the right. Follow the road as it curves left and then follow it, straight ahead, towards High Applegarth.

From here the splendid scar reveals its glory. Ash and yew

grow crag-fast and larch and hawthorns scatter the slope. You might see a sparrowhawk flying fast over the vegetation, hoping to make a kill of one of the many songbirds that nest on the slopes.

Look for the stile in the fence on the left just before the farm and stride on the well-waymarked path, part of the Coast to Coast Walk. Once you are past the monuments high above, look for evidence of an ancient Iron Age fort - perhaps just a green hump. Pass through the gate and continue through glorious deciduous woodland, where you might be tempted to do more birdwatching. Beyond the exit gate you rapidly approach High Lease Farm, where you left the track earlier. From now on it is generally downhill all the way to rejoin your car.

ALONG THE WAY:

Robert Willance lived and died at 24 Frenchgate in Richmond. One day, while he was hunting on horseback on Whitcliffe Scar, the mist came down. He spurred his horse into hurrying home and the mare leapt over the scar, plunging 200 ft. Sadly the horse was killed but, miraculously, Robert survived, losing only his leg. He became an alderman of the town in 1608 and in gratitude for his survival he presented a chalice to the corporation. He died in 1616 and was buried in the churchyard of St Mary, Frenchgate.

While in Richmond, children might like to hunt for the plaque commemorating Robert and seeking his gravestone.

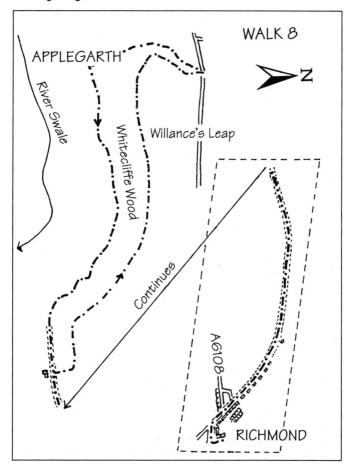

33

WALK 9:
RICHMOND TO EASBY ABBEY

Richmond is a grand town. It has a huge cobbled horseshoe-shaped market place at the centre of which stands the chapel of the Holy Trinity, founded in or about 1135. A huge obelisk rears upwards, built on the site of a medieval cross. Towering over the pleasing houses and shops which surround the market place is the great Norman keep of the castle built by Alan Rufus in 1071 to protect himself from the Saxons. It was built on precipitous crags rising from the River Swale. In 1782 Castle Walk was built as a fashionable Georgian promenade to take advantage of the splendid views.

Start: Market Square, Richmond. GR.172008.
Total distance: 4km (2½ miles).
Height gain: 30m (100 feet).
Difficulty: Easy walking except for steep climbs down to and up from the river.

THE WALK:

Leave the Market Place by the side of the Town Hall Hotel. Bear left along Tower Street until a flight of steps is reached. Join the roadway and drop down the steep narrow road to the falls and the riverside (The 'Batts'), where you will want to enjoy the magnificent falls. Return up the road for a hundred yards and turn right into Riverside Road, where you veer right down Park Wynd. Continue along the footpath, with a good view of the fine arched gritstone bridge over the Swale.

Cross Station Road and continue along Lombards Wynd. Turn right along Easby Low Road, an unsurfaced lane signposted Easby Abbey, and continue up into Clink Bank Wood, with fine retrospective

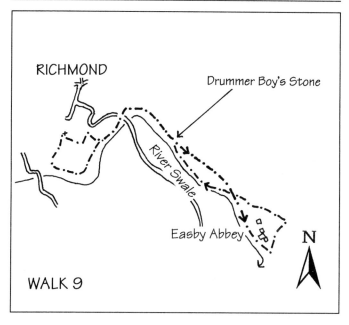

RICHMOND

Drummer Boy's Stone

River Swale

Easby Abbey

N

WALK 9

views of Richmond. As the lane drops down join the upper of two paths.

Look for the Drummer Boy Stone, a slab wedged behind the gatepost of a four-bar gate on your left. A drummer boy was supposed to have been lowered, by soldiers, below the obelisk in the market place and told to find his way along underground passages believed to exist between the castle and Easby Abbey. Legend has it that the boy was never seen again but occasionally people say they have heard a drum beat. The slab marks the last place the soldiers heard the drum.

Continue along the lovely path for about half a mile. Beyond the stile keep along the riverside path to pass Abbey Mill, a former corn mill. Stride on to enter and explore the extensive ruins of Easby Abbey.

Continue on along the lane to visit the lovely little church of St Agatha of Sicily. Go on and climb a short slope to take a track leading left. A short way along is a waymarked stile on the left. Continue across the pasture, with a good view of the castle ahead, to a stile into woodland.

Descend the steps beyond to the side of the Swale and return through the trees to climb up the lane taken earlier. Return to walk Riverside Road and turn up right to the steps, now on your left, along Castle Walk. This takes you below the castle walls, with a sheer drop to the Swale.

The views are incomparable with Green Bridge, and The Green far below, and Billy Bank Woods beyond. As you continue round you can see Culloden Tower, built in 1746 by John Yorke to mark the Duke of Cumberland's defeat of Bonnie Prince Charlie.

Continue on the walk to return to the Market Place.

ALONG THE WAY:

Easby Abbey was founded in 1155 by Roald, Constable of Richmond Castle. In the time of Edward III, it came into the possession of the Scropes, lords of Bolton. The abbey suffered from frequent Scottish raids during the Middle Ages. Ironically, great damage was caused in 1346 when the English army was billeted nearby on its way to the battle of Neville's Cross. In the late 1530s Henry VIII dissolved all monasteries.

The ruins of the abbey are a grand place for youngsters to explore but they are asked not to climb on the walls.

The Church of St Agatha, a Sicilian saint martyred in the 3rd-century, is a Norman foundation. Enjoy its splendid 14th-century porch and look for the various coats of arms, including that of the Scropes. In the chancel is a large piscina and three trefoiled stone seats. Its greatest treasure is perhaps the wonderful 13th-century wall paintings. Children will enjoy trying to identify the biblical pictures.

WALK 10:
LADY ANNE'S HIGHWAY
AND THE RISE OF THE RIVER URE

The River Ure rises on the wild moorland of Ure Head. It trickles steadily, descends as a stream, hides for a short distance underground, and crosses Lady Anne's Highway. This pleasingly-named track forms the spine of this delightful walk, which takes in a diminutive church, comes close to the Carlisle to Settle railway and crosses Hell Gill. Young people should approach the latter with care.

Start: A lay-by close to Shotlock Tunnel on the B6259. GR.788943.
Total distance: 6km (4 miles).
Height gain: 66m (217 feet).
Difficulty: Easy walking all the way but expect lots of mud after rain.

THE WALK:

From the lay-by on the B-road, walk south to the western corner of Lunds Wood. Continue on to take a signposted stile on the left. Walk diagonally left to pass through three stone gap stiles and then straddle another stile into a cleared area at the edge of the wood. Climb the stile opposite, bear right and follow a path through conifers to a stile to a track. Turn right to stride the wide way, following the sign for Lunds. Cross the Ure and follow the signposted directions to the church.

The tiny church was built in the early 18th-century. It served a very scattered parish. The unmarked graves, among which sheep and lambs graze, are probably those of navvies who died during the construction of the railway (1871 to 1876).

Leave this quiet corner by a small wooden gate in the wall on the left. Cross a narrow bridge over a beck and continue, keeping parallel with it, to a gated gap in the next wall. Go on in front of a farmhouse and climb to another plank bridge. Beyond another gated gap. climb a very

37

steep slope to Shaws - which later became a youth hostel. Cross yet another footbridge and climb moss-covered steps out of the hollow to a gate. Turn left and walk the signposted way for The Highway, ascending a wide sloping track. Continue where it comes close to a wall, climb the stile in the wall ahead and turn left to walk north along the track.

The Highway is named after the 17th-century Lady Anne Clifford, who inherited the castles of Appleby, Brough, Brougham, Skipton and Pendragon. After repairing and rebuilding the castles she spent the latter part of her life visiting them, driving along the old road in her four-wheeled carriage, and caring for the needs of her tenants.

Step out along the track, past the ruins of the aptly-named High Hall, which stands beside Washer Gill. Ford the small beck and take the lower way. Cross another small stream and then the young Ure. The track then sweeps on towards Hell Gill, and crosses it by Hell Gill Bridge. Below in the depths rages another infant beck, which soon becomes the River Eden.

The Highway was once so busy with travellers that it attracted highwaymen. One, nick-named 'Swift Nicks', was reputed to have leapt across Hell Gill on his grey horse on the way to the inn at High Dike. A cottage attached to the inn was once Lunds School.

After peeping with care over the parapet of the bridge to see the awesome gill, turn round and begin your return by the wide grassy swathe by which you reached the bridge. Ignore The Highway and continue on the steadily descending way, with a dramatic view of the forbidding slopes of Baugh Fell to your right. Look for the well-preserved limekiln on your left and then the young Ure dropping, white-topped, over several limestone outcrops before it continues on its way. Descend steadily to cross Green Bridge, a tractor crossing over the sweetly sing-ing Ure. Beyond, the stream continues its journey south through an area known as Ure Crook. Follow the track to cross a now wider Ure on the sturdy stone How Beck Bridge. Stroll on to Shaw Paddock, where the track joins the B-road by the railway bridge. At the road, turn left to rejoin your car.

ALONG THE WAY:

The River Ure springs on Ure Head, an area much wilder and more lonely than the country-side it meanders through by the time it has reached Hawes. From this small market town it flows

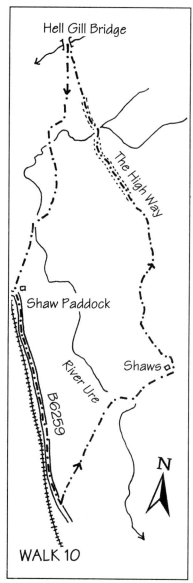

Hell Gill Bridge

The High Way

Shaw Paddock

River Ure

B6259

Shaws

N

WALK 10

steadily, through meadows, for mile after mile. Villages lie close to it, or sit on terraces above the lovely river. Near Aysgarth the Ure changes character and descends exuberantly, for 200 feet, over great ledges of limestone in three sets of impressive falls, before surging on. At Myton-on-Swale, the Ure joins the Swale to become the River Ouse, which in turn flows into the Humber Estuary and the North Sea.

The River Eden which, as a small stream hurried through Hell Gill and came so close to the Ure, soon turns north, diverted long ago by glacial drift, and surges through the Eden Valley, emptying its waters into the Solway and the Irish Sea.

The B6259 from the Moorcock Inn to Shaw Paddock was constructed in 1825, replacing The Highway. The track through the conifers to Lunds church and the bridge over the Ure were constructed by a Mr Scott Macfie who lived at Shaws, a house high on the slopes. The track and the bridge made the church more accessible and saved the parishioners from fording the beck.

WALK 11:
HAWES TO HARDRAW

Walking from Hawes to Hardraw, visiting the lovely hill hamlets of Sedbusk and Simonstone, is a delightful way of introducing young people to the pleasures of Wensleydale. The walk has many paved trods to traverse, numerous squeeze stiles to pass through, a magnificent waterfall to view and a pleasing road bridge and a gem of a packhorse bridge to cross. It starts and ends at Hawes, often called T'Haas after its original name The Hawes. The charming market town sits at the head of Wensleydale and has many interesting shops to visit. The whole family will enjoy a free visit to the ropeworks to see a ropewalk. It is close to the station car park.

Start: National Park Centre Car Park at the old Hawes station. Pay and display. GR.876898.
Total distance: 6km (4 miles).
Height gain: 60m (197 feet).
Difficulty: Easy: a very satisfactory walk, and a real family favourite.

THE WALK:

Within the car park, cross the old railway and climb up the stepped slope to Brunt Acres Road. Walk right for 75 yards. At the entrance to Hawes rural workshops, on the left, take the Pennine Way signposted stile to walk a paved trod through two pastures to rejoin the road.

These flagged paths, firmly embedded in the ground, would have been used by lead miners, coal miners and quarrymen. They led to limekilns. They have been used by generations of walkers and have prevented the grass from becoming worn on either side.

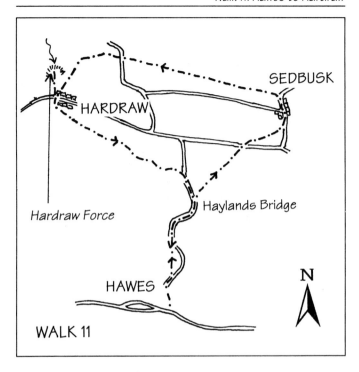

SEDBUSK

HARDRAW

Hardraw Force

Haylands Bridge

HAWES

N

WALK 11

Cross the twin-arched Haylands Bridge, built in 1820, over the wide River Ure. Look here for flood holes in the base of the walls, on either side of the river. When the Ure is in spate and it spills over its banks the flood water runs away through the holes, breaking the force of the water. Walk on to take the stile, signposted Sedbusk, on the right and go on to cross an isolated, cobbled packhorse bridge over a small stream. Ascend the clear way to cross the narrow lane to Askrigg and climb the stile opposite. Bear right, where you are asked to walk in single file, and continue over pastures to a stile on to Sedbusk Lane, where you turn left and then right into the small hamlet.

Sedbusk is a small village of sturdy gritstone houses, which sits on a ridge below Abbotside Common. Shutt Lane, climbing out of the village, led to limekilns, quarries and lead mines.

Walk beside the tiny green

and then cross it, left, to take a squeeze stile. Walk ahead. From now on, the level walk westwards is through a series of squeeze stiles (17 in all, including two ladderstiles) with magnificent views over the wide dale of Wensley to Wether Fell and one of its buttresses, Yorburgh. At Simonstone, a tiny hamlet, turn left and almost immediately right, to walk a fenced track towards Simonstone Hall, an elegant country hotel, which welcomes walkers. This was once the shooting lodge of the Earl of Wharncliffe.

Opposite the main gate, take the gated stile on your left to begin the steepish descent, over flagged paths, to the village of Hardraw. Turn right into the Green Dragon public house, the only approach to Hardraw Force.

Pay your admission and walk the path, beside Fossdale Beck to see the magnificent Force, a 96 foot single drop, the highest unbroken waterfall in England. Here you are asked to be responsible for your own safety and not to walk behind the waterfall. Adventurous children should follow their parents' advice.

Return to the main street, which you cross, to take a Pennine Way signposted stile, to the right of the Coach House Café. Turn left to walk the flagged way, passing through nine more squeeze stiles, to reach Brunt Acres Road, just above woodland. Turn right and follow your outward route.

ALONG THE WAY:

Hardraw Force: This is Wensleydale's spectacular attraction. Fossdale Beck descends over Hardraw Scar. The lip is limestone of the Yoredale series and, below this, sandstone. The deep plunge pool is backed by shale and the force of the water has eaten away this softer rock, forming caves. Over the years the water of the beck steadily erodes the lip. In 1899 a great storm over Shunner Fell, above, sent a tremendous flood down the ravine and washed away the lip. An artificial one was put in its place by the workmen of the Earl of Wharncliffe.

To the left of the path to the waterfall stands the Church of St Mary and St John, rebuilt in 1880 by the earl. It was often featured in the TV series *All Creatures Great and Small.*

Between the church and the force is a walled enclosure, a bandstand. Here brass band concerts take place and the amphitheatre of rock provides superb acoustics.

WALK 12:
ASKRIGG TO BAINBRIDGE

The limestone fells slope back from the lovely Dales town of Askrigg and quiet walled pastures creep right up to its outskirts. Brownstone houses of the 17th- and 18th-century tightly line the main street. The town was the setting for the TV series *All Creatures Great and Small*. Children will enjoy looking for Skeldale House, now an Abbeyfield home, which was the home and surgery of Herriot's vet in the programme. "Darrowby" market cross, close by St Oswald's church, is where this glorious walk starts.

Start: St Oswald's Church. GR.948910.
Total distance: 9½km (6 miles).
Height gain: 110m (420 feet).
Difficulty: Easy walking all the way except for the descent to the foot of Whitfield Gill Force.

THE WALK:

Before you leave the market square, visit the large late-Perpendicular church, the "Cathedral of Wensleydale", which dates from about 1450. Enjoy the splendid wooden-beamed ceiling of its nave and its fine glass windows. Spend time looking at the lichen-encrusted gravestones, engraved with names and occupations. Many of those remembered were clockmakers, because Askrigg was renowned for its hand-made clocks. A clock-maker lacking a tool would design and fashion it to do the job.

Leave the square by West End, following the signpost for Mill Gill Force. Continue along the lane and take the signposted footpath on the right to walk a paved path across a buttercup meadow towards a mill.

The waters of the gill once powered three mills. The one

you pass was for corn and later generated electricity for Askrigg. The mill below was first for cotton and then flax, the lowest began as a woollen mill.

Cross a tiny footbridge and turn right to enter glorious beech woodland by a signposted gate. Away to the left is a good view of the dramatic outline of Addlebrough. Follow the well-signposted way, passing through capacious kissing gates, remembering those Victorian crinolined ladies who also walked this way. At the signpost, take the lower path into the sheer-sided ravine. Ahead lies the magnificent waterfall, which descends through a deep cleft in the huge amphitheatre of rock. Visit in the morning when the long streams of droplets sparkle and shimmer in sunshine.

Return to the signpost and follow the directions for Whitfield Gill Force, walking a path bordered with violets and bluebells. Pass through stiled and waymarked pastures with ewes and lambs. Take a gap stile in the wall on your right and continue along another high-level path above the beck. Leave by a stile on the left and walk to a stepped stile under a huge ash. (Note this stile for your return.) Beyond, walk the clear way towards the gill. Keep to the upper path, close by the boundary wall, each time the path divides, until you are well clear of an exceedingly soft muddy area. Then descend, with care, the steepish slope to the side of the beck to see a tremendous curtain of water descending for thirty feet over an unbreached amphitheatre into the secluded gill, the haunt of many small songbirds.

This is an exciting corner for children to clamber about boulders but they should be reminded how slippery they can be.

To continue, return to the stile below the ash. Just before it, strike diagonally right up the slope to the corner of a wall and then walk ahead (west), across the pasture, to pass through a signposted gate gap. Turn left and follow the wall downhill to take a gate to the left of a dwelling at the hamlet of Helm (pronounced Hellum).

Join Skelgill Lane and bear left to walk downhill towards Grange. Look over the wall on the right to see a magnificent fall on Grange Beck and then a charming arched bridge over more cascades.

At Bow Bridge, turn left and after 100 yds take a flagged footpath on the right.

Pass beside the farmhouse and the remains of an old chapel, to cross a very narrow

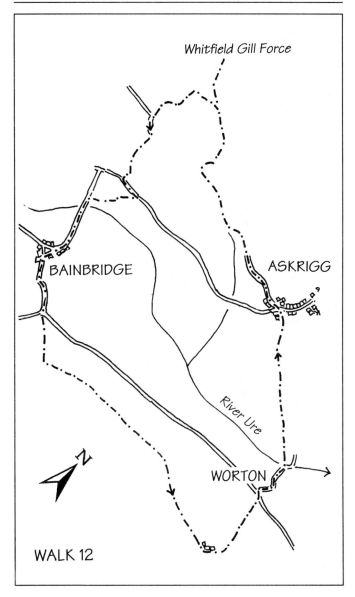

Whitfield Gill Force

BAINBRIDGE

ASKRIGG

River Ure

N

WORTON

WALK 12

45

packhorse bridge.

Turn left and walk between the remnants of a disused railway bridge and follow, right, the continuing paved footpath to Yore Bridge over the River Ure. Turn left and stroll into the charming village of Bainbridge, walking between its spacious greens to cross Bain Bridge, where the very short river comes over its bed in a long series of spectacular falls.

Stride on, passing Brough Hill, the site of a fort occupied by the Romans for 300 years. Take the first right turn and then the signposted stile on the left. Strike diagonally right over stiled pastures to climb to Brough Scar. Turn left and walk the high-level way until you reach the signpost for Cubeck, which you follow. Walk diagonally right on the stiled way to pass right of the farm and continue to a narrow lane. Turn left and step the glorious way to Worton. Cross the A-road with care and go through the quiet hamlet to a bridge across the Ure.

Take the signposted path on the left, which soon becomes flagged, across the meadows to Askrigg. The path joins a narrow lane, which swings left and returns you to the market cross.

ALONG THE WAY:

Fors Abbey: Peter de Quincey, a monk from Brittany, wanted to form a Cistercian abbey. He chose a site above the packhorse bridge and near to the farmhouse by Bow Bridge, passed on the walk. Fors Abbey was the first in Wensleydale. It survived for about eleven years in spite of the exposed position, difficult terrain, attacks by wolves and plunder by local people. It was then transferred to pastures near East Witton and became Jervaulx Abbey. The bridge over the cascades on Grange Beck, seen on the walk, has been attributed to the monks of the abbey. The disused railway was cut through the burial ground and many bones were found.

WALK 13:
COUNTERSETT AND SEMERWATER

This exhilarating walk poviding delightful views and lots of historical interest, is centred on the picturesque village of Bainbridge, once an important Roman garrison. Troops occupied its fort on Brough Hill for 300 years. In the first century AD, Emperor Agricola built a road leading west from the village over Wether Fell and on to Ribblehead. Today a rough track, known as Cam High Road, follows the course of the original Roman road.

Below the village of Countersett stands Semerwater, a tranquil lake, tree-fringed and lying in a lovely hollow in the hills. On its shore can be seen some large boulders, 'erratics' deposited here at the end of the last Ice Age.

Start: On the west side of Bainbridge's village green. GR.934903.
Total distance: 8km (5 miles).
Height gain: 220m (750 feet).
Difficulty: Generally easy. Steady climb to Hawes End and over Bracken Fell.

THE WALK:

Leave the village green by the signposted road to Marsett, passing the Temperance Hall on the right.

As you climb steadily, notice that the wall on the right has four rows of throughs, which give it added strength.

Where the road turns sharp left, stride ahead along the Roman road, Cam High Road, which stretches straight ahead for as far as you can see. From this gradually ascending airy rough track notice the pleasing field patterns created by sturdy walls, many pastures complete with their own characteristic barns. After one and a half miles, turn sharp left to continue up Countersett Road. Where the

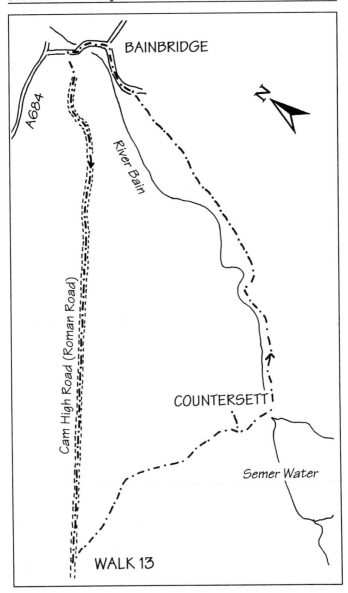

BAINBRIDGE

A684

River Bain

Cam High Road (Roman Road)

N

COUNTERSETT

Semer Water

WALK 13

road makes another sharp swing, right, take the footpath on the left, signposted Countersett: ½ mile. As you descend to a stile, keeping beside the wall, you have a first delightful glimpse of the lake. Beyond, drop downhill for a short distance and then veer left to another stile. Keep to the right of a barn beyond. Continue downhill to cross a small stream to walk left of another barn, passing through a gate. Descend to a gate to a track, bear right and continue ahead to a signpost.

Turn left and look left to see several beeboles in the wall of a cottage. Walk on a few steps to see Countersett Hall, the meeting house and the old school. Continue to the end of the delightful hamlet.

Return to the signpost and follow the directions for Stalling Busk. Go down the quiet lane to cross the charming three-arched Semerwater Bridge.

To see a group of Shap granite boulders near the water's edge walk on. These are known as the Carlhow Stone and the Mermaids Stones and were carried here by glacier.

Take the stile on the left beyond the bridge. The stile is signposted Bainbridge: 2 miles. The walk runs beside the River Bain, often described as England's shortest river. In less than two miles it unites with the River Ure. The stiled way is easy to follow. Just after half a mile the path moves away from the river to a ladderstile over the wall. From here climb a wide grassy way to continue over Bracken Hill. Remember to look back for a grand view of Raydale.

Follow the stiled way and then begin the gradual descent over glorious green trods towards Bainbridge. Continue beside the road wall on your right to reach the main road, just below Brough Hill. Turn left to cross the bridge. Pause here to enjoy the magnificent falls on the Bain as it rages on its way to add its energy to the Ure.

ALONG THE WAY:
Semerwater: Although Semerwater owes its existence to the Ice Age, legend tells another story about its formation.

Once a beautiful city stood where the water now lies. An angel visited it disguised as a beggar. At each house he asked for food but was roughly turned away, except at a mean cottage outside the city. Here a poor man and his wife took him in and fed him. Next day a terrible noise was heard and the city sank and was covered with water, all except the tiny cottage.

WALK 14:

AYSGARTH TO BOLTON CASTLE

Everyone should visit the splendid Aysgarth Falls. In spate they are magnificent. This walk passes the middle and lower falls, with delightful views across the river to the church. There are pleasing viewing platforms from which the whole family can see the tempestuous river, though you should take good notice of the National Park's advice not to stray from the platforms. The walk then passes over meadows, climbing steadily to the forbidding Bolton Castle, an exciting place for children to visit, with its great towers and crenellations. The walk returns over rolling countryside.

Start: Aysgarth Falls National Park Centre. GR.012887.
Total distance: 9½km (6 miles).
Height gain: 120m (390 feet).
Difficulty: A pleasing walk over pastures.

THE WALK:

Leave the National Park Centre by the fenced path to the road, and cross it with care. Enter Freeholders' Wood and continue ahead on the hard path to visit first the middle falls and then the lower, all well-signposted.

Return to the hard path and walk back for a few yards to take the footpath, now on your right, signposted Castle Bolton. Beyond the first stile you walk through a pasture called The Riddings. Follow the stiled way. Head across a pasture towards Hollins House Farm.

Go through a gate and follow the track through the farm, to join a reinforced track along which you continue. Leave it by a sign-post, right, beyond a chicken house, and carry on to pass through a stile in the wall. Follow the signpost (north-east) for Castle Bolton, now just in view.

Descend to the next stile, by a gate. Bear right, with the wall to your left, and go on through two more stiles. Walk on in the direction of the signpost: the track is indistinct.

There are so many signposts, waymarks, yellow blobs and stiles that children will enjoy finding the way, with the castle ahead to keep them in the right direction.

Pass another signpost and step across a stream - which might require wading if the beck is in spate - and go on to join Thoresby Lane, a hedged and sometimes muddy track, by a stile. Stroll the long, lovely way to join a metalled lane at Low Thoresby. Walk on to cross Beldon Beck, sometimes a fast-flowing stream, by a tractor bridge. Take the easy-to-miss step stile immediately on the left. Go through a broken wall and turn right, ignoring the private stile in front of you. Ahead, the castle towers upwards. Walk to the far right corner of the pasture to an obscured stile and, beyond, stride to the road. Turn left and walk for 300 yards to follow a path on the right. This takes you up to a dismantled railway and on to join the road to the castle and the pleasant village of Castle Bolton.

After visiting the village, church and castle, walk west along the road between the castle and the church, to take the stile on the left, signposted Aysgarth. Pass, by stiles, through a narrow strip of woodland and continue half-left across a large pasture of lynchets to a gate, half-way along the wall opposite. Follow the waymarked telegraph poles to a gated stile ahead. Drop down to cross a footbridge over Beldon Beck in its pretty tree-lined gill. Climb right, to a stile in the wall. Follow the waymarked fence posts on your right to a gated stile in front of West Bolton Farm.

Pass to the left of the farm and take two waymarked stiles beyond, the farm's access track bearing sharp left. Climb the slope to a stile beside the far corner of a wood on your left. Walk half-left to cross a small beck and then stride beside it to a stile ahead.

Head on the stiled way (no instructions are needed), which joins a track leading down towards East End Farm.

Just beyond the gate to the farm, turn sharp left, and make your way to a stile to the road.

Turn right to walk into Carperby. Take the signposted way, on the left, opposite the Wheatsheaf Inn. Cross a small stream, bear right through a gate and then continue with the wall to your left to a stile to Low Lane.

Cross, and take the stile

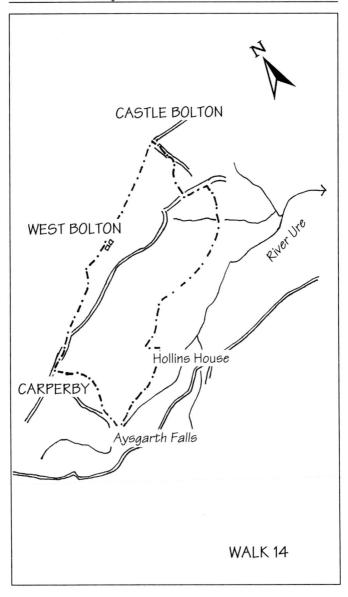

WALK 14

opposite. Walk down beside the wall on your right and take the signposted gap on your right, before the hedge. Strike diagonally across the pasture to a stile near the right corner. Follow the line of stiles to re-enter Freeholders' Wood. Cross a track and continue in the same general direction to join the road. Pass under the railway bridge to return to the National Park Centre.

ALONG THE WAY:

River Ure: The River Ure flows quietly until it reaches Aysgarth, where it descends 50m (200 feet) by the Aysgarth Falls, to flow through Lower Wensleydale. The underlying layers of shale have been eroded by the river and have undercut the limestone, creating a series of steps in the river bed.

Freeholder's Wood: is managed as a coppiced woodland by the National Park. It is divided into plots, and approximately, every 15 years, in rotation, the trees are cut back to stump level. Once this would have provided timber for fencing, firewood, and laths. Today it provides an ideal habitat for nesting birds. The Riddings is a field, so named after it was cleared, or 'rid', of scrub by medieval farmers.

Bolton Castle: was built in the reign of Richard II by Richard le Scrope. Mary, Queen of Scots, was held prisoner here for six months. In the Civil War it was held for the king and withstood a lengthy siege but was captured by the Parliamentarians and dismantled in 1647. Leave time to visit its halls, chambers, monk's cell, armourer's forge, ale house, threshing floor, dungeon and battlements.

Carperby: was a centre of Quakerism and was visited by George Fox on his preaching tours. It is also the 'birthplace' of the breed of sheep known as Wensleydales.

WALK 15:
WEST BURTON TO WEST WITTON

The village of West Burton lies at the foot of Wasset Fell.
The latter divides two charming side dales of Wensleydale.
They are Bishopdale, wide-floored, where once there was a
glacial lake, and Waldendale, a lonely, deep V-shaped valley
through which flows Walden Beck. The lovely impetuous
stream continues past West Burton and unites with
Bishopdale Beck before the two add their waters to the
River Ure.
Children will enjoy striding the old packhorse route of this
walk, from which there are some tremendous views; look
for villages lying along the sides of Wensleydale, tucked
under the friendly hills. The walk begins and ends in West
Burton and time should be allowed to explore it.

Start: From the village green, West Burton. GR.019867.
Total distance: 11½km (7 miles).
Height gain: 216m (709 feet).
Difficulty: Generally easy: pleasant walking on tracks. Steep descent to
West Burton.

THE WALK:

Turn left at the bottom of the village green and walk on to join the B6160. Cross Burton Bridge on your right, an old packhorse bridge over the Walden Beck. It is signposted: 'Weak Bridge'. Beyond, stride the walled lane, an ancient highway believed to have been a Roman road from Bainbridge to Middleham. Pass Flanders Hall, with its sturdy mounting block and decorated chimneys. Beyond you have the first of many good views of Bolton Castle. Stroll on past Howraine Farm and follow the track, steep and unsurfaced, now called Morpeth Gate. Away to your right tower the fine limestone slopes of Penhill. Ignore all other footpaths off the track until you come to a stile on your left signposted Templars Chapel: 1 mile. Beyond, go ahead over pasture to a signpost directing you along the upper way. Below you can see a large house, called Sorrelsykes, once the home of Elizabeth Montague, the essayist. Bear left and then carry on the well-waymarked stiled way, with magnificent views of Wensleydale to your left. Cross a track coming up from the valley. Beyond are the fenced ruins of Penhill Preceptory, an ancient chapel.

Leave the chapel by the stile and climb diagonally to a small wood at the top of the same field.

On the far side of the dale look for Cobscar chimney and Keld Heads chimney - almost two miles apart - between which stretched an underground flue carrying away noxious substances from both mines.

Beyond a metal gate by the wood stands a stone, with carvings, fixed to a large slate, possibly once part of the preceptory. Ahead in the distance you can glimpse the North Yorkshire Moors.

Continue to a concrete track, where you turn right. After a hundred yards take the grassy path on the left, signposted Nossill Lane, which climbs steeply up the slope to a gate. Climb the gap stile beside it and walk ahead, keeping parallel with the limestone wall on your left. Go on through the next pasture and then take the signposted gated stile in the wall on your right to join Langthwaite Lane, a wide, walled track with thorn bushes on either side. Above to your right lie Nossill Scars. Go on as the way steadily descends to join Green Gate Lane, and turn left.

Carry on below woodland to take a footpath on the right, before the first house in West Witton. Here you might wish to visit the village before continuing. The narrow path climbs through the trees and then continues directly ahead from a stile through a caravan site to a gate and a plank footbridge across a stream. Climb left up the slope and look over the fence to see West Witton's charming waterfall. Head across the pasture to a gated stile. Beyond, strike diagonally across more pasture to the near side of a barn to join a track along which you continue. In fifty yards, take a stile in the wall on your right. Strike ahead to another stile in the far right corner. Beyond is another delightful fall, beside which you climb, on the right side of the tumbling stream. Pass

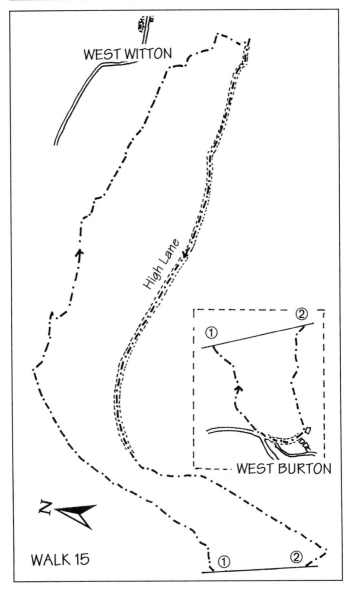

WEST WITTON

High Lane

WEST BURTON

① ②

N

WALK 15

① ②

through the stile and turn right to return along High Lane, walked earlier, and then called Morpeth Gate.

As you stroll this glorious way, high up on the slopes of Penhill, you feel you can hear the noise of the cattle that were once driven along it.

After two miles, at Morpeth Gate, take the upper track signposted: West Burton. The way goes on and on until you reach a board that instructs you to turn sharp right. Descend over the slopes of Knarlton Knot to pass through a signposted gated stile in the fell wall. Beyond, walk left to follow the steep zigzagging way-marked narrow path, down the scar. Beyond a gap stile, bear slightly right along the edge of Barrack Wood to take a stile in the fence on the left. Bear right from the stile to cross the next pasture and continue with the wall to your left. Follow the stiled way to walk down the paved walled path, to stand on another packhorse bridge, with low parapets, to view the charming West Burton Falls. Turn right from the bridge and then left to return to the village green.

ALONG THE WAY:

West Burton: has houses along both sides of a large village green. On the green stands a spired stone cross with steps leading up to it. Close by are stocks, swings and a slide, linking the old with the new. The village was built to house miners and quarrymen. Today the houses and cottages have been attractively restored and there is an inn and two shops.

Walden Beck: The lovely water-fall where the walk ended is some-times known as Cauldron Falls. Here Walden Beck has cut its way through a wooded gorge before descending a limestone amphitheatre.

West Witton: has houses on either side of a long street, behind which the limestone crags of Penhill stand up like battlements. It is another village that grew to house miners. Once it had a Norman church but this was rebuilt in the 19th-century. The villagers buried their dead in Wensley churchyard, unable to find enough soil in their own, until abut 1780 when soil was carted in.

Swinithwaite Hall: In 1840 a curious mound above Swinithwaite Hall intrigued its owner. He excavated and dis-covered the foundations of a chapel, fragments of armour, bases of pillars, two small cof-fins and some worn steps. It was a chapel of the Knights Templar, built around 1200.

WALK 16:
MIDDLEHAM TO COVERHAM ABBEY

From either end of Wensleydale, Middleham is reached by a hill. It is a wonderful place to start a walk and time should be allowed for exploring. Visit the castle; look for the two squares, both with a market cross; find the memorial to Queen Victoria and read the plaques commemorating highlights of her life; find the old school with a tower; wander over the cobbled alleys; go to the church dedicated to a Saxon saint who was strangled by two Danish women.

Middleham was once the home of a king and is renowned in the racing world for the breeding and training of horses. From this delightful small town the walk takes you into the peace and quiet of Coverdale, where there is much of interest.

Start: The lower, cobbled square at Middleham. GR.128878.
Total distance: 7.25km (4½ miles).
Height gain: Virtually none.
Difficulty: An easy walk.

THE WALK:

From the square go uphill for a short distance and turn left up a cobbled way, between houses set back behind others. Continue along the signposted lane, with the castle to your right. Just before the gate, take a waymarked gated stile on the right and head diagonally left to a gate in a fence. Stride over the next pasture for a detour to see the motte and bailey earthworks on William's Hill. This is the site of an early Norman building. From the top there is a grand view of the castle.

Return to the gate on the lane and pass through. Continue up the slope, with the wall to your right. Pass through the waymarked gate and go on with the wall now to your left. Near where a boundary wall, coming from the left, meets the wall to your left, go diagonally right to the field corner between a copse of pines on your left and a barn on your right (no waymark to tell you where to strike across). Use the two stiles to pass through the tip of the copse and then drop steadily downhill, with a good view of Penhill ahead. Descend the cart track beneath beech and ash towards the delightful River Cover. Look here for nuthatches, tree creepers, and long-tailed and blue tits.

Cross the charming Hullo Bridge and continue uphill on a track, a bridleway, which leads you to Hanghow Lane and the entrance to Braithwaite Hall.

This 17th-century manor house, which still has some original oak panelling, was built by Benjamin Purchas. It was bequeathed to the National trust in 1940 and is now a working farmhouse, open for visits by appointment.

Go right along the walled lane and begin your descent

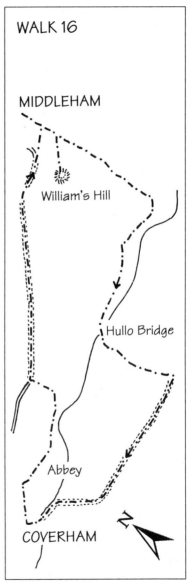

WALK 16

MIDDLEHAM

William's Hill

Hullo Bridge

Abbey

COVERHAM

N

into the lovely Coverdale. Cross the high-arched Coverham Bridge, where you may see more nuthatches. Turn right to walk along a track, passing a dwelling on the left, once a mill. It was built by monks. Take the gate on the left, just beyond the former mill-race, and climb up by the hurrying water to visit the 13th-century church of the Holy Trinity.

The church was in use until the 1970s and was the church for all who lived in the dale of the River Cover. Today the vale has few buildings and the church is maintained by the Redundant Churches fund. In the Middle Ages lead and coal mines contributed to the prosperity of the neighbourhood and quarries were worked for stone, used for millstones. Then the church would have been full of parishioners from its extensive parish. Holy Trinity lies close to Coverham Abbey, which is typical of most monasteries in having a parish church at its gate.

Return to the track and walk on to pass under the arch of the inner gatehouse and then past the pleasant house on the right, built onto the remains of part of the abbey.

As you continue, children might like to spot the many carved stones, figures, grave slabs, pieces of window frames and pillars incorporated into gardens and buildings and even a wall of the farm. Sad though it is to see parts of the abbey fabric so scattered, the wonderful peace and sheer beauty of the abbey's surroundings make it a joy to walk.

Carry on ahead along the continuing grassy track, following the signpost for Pinkers Pond. Walk on through the pastures, with the river to your right. Pass to the right of a small ruin and then climb up a slope behind another building. At a small wood ahead, turn left and continue up the slope to the road. Turn right on to Coverham Lane. Opposite lies the attractive large pond, a family favourite for a picnic. Continue along the high-level lane, using the wide grass verge, well out of the way of vehicular traffic. Look out for racehorses, using the same verge, as you enjoy the magnificent views of Wensleydale.

At the sign for Middleham take the stile on the right and walk the stiled way beside the wall on your left to return to the lane beside the castle taken on your outward route.

WALK 17:
LEYBURN TO WENSLEY

The village that gives its name to Wensleydale is quiet and unobtrusive now but was once an important market town. Most dales are named after their river, so you might expect this one to be named Uredale or Yoredale. That did not sound right, but Wensleydale did. Edward I granted Wensley a charter in 1306 but in 1563 it was devastated by plague and it never recovered. Its market and trade went to Leyburn, then a hamlet in the parish of Wensley. Later, Charles II granted Leyburn a market charter. This walk is full of interest for all the family. It starts from a lively spacious town, continues high along a limestone scarp, passes by remnants of Wensleydale's largest lead mine, visits one of the most impressive churches in the dale, and returns over quiet pastures ideal for birdwatching.

Start: Town Hall in the market place, Leyburn. GR.112905.
Total distance: 9km (5½ miles).
Height gain: 60m (197 feet).
Difficulty: Easy walking on good clear tracks.

THE WALK:

From the Town Hall, walk towards the top of the market place (west). Cross the A684 and continue on, passing to the right of the Dalesman's Club, following 'A way to the Shawl' sign. At the street end, turn left and go through a kissing gate on your right. Walk on along a flagged way and continue climbing steadily along the edge of the scarp with panoramic views up Wensleydale. The magnificent Penhill dominates all.

This natural terrace, 800 feet

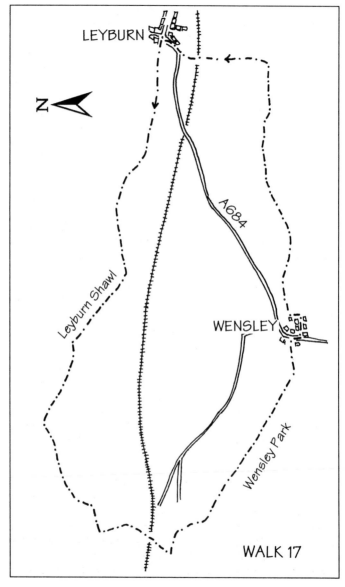

LEYBURN

N

A684

Leyburn Shawl

WENSLEY

Wensley Park

WALK 17

above sea level and extending for two miles, is known as Leyburn Shawl. The name shawl perhaps originates from the Anglo-Saxon 'schale', meaning easily splitting rock. Or it could have come from a corruption of the Norse word 'skali', which means hut. Local legend says it is named after the shawl of Mary Queen of Scots, which she dropped as she fled along the escarpment from Bolton Castle, where she was imprisoned. The Victorians had tea festivals on the 'shawl'; in 1845 more than a thousand people had tea in a grand marquee and more than two thousand joined in the dancing.

Continue through a stile to follow a path above the wood. Stay on the ridge top. Ignore a track that leads diagonally left down the scarp. Go on along the rim of the scarp just inside Warren Wood and on reaching a wire fence at the edge of the trees climb the stile and take the next stile ahead. Beyond drop down the slope to a waymarked stile to the left of a gate. Stride on to pass scattered boulders and depressions in the ground, part of an ancient settlement and field system. Join a farm track and follow it downhill and left to a junction where you bear right. Walk on to pass Tullis Cote Farmhouse on your left.

At the next gate, notice the arched stone barn, once a peat store for Keld Head Mine, over which you have been walking. Turn left and walk down the track, which soon becomes metalled as you pass a huge chimney and the engine shed of the old mine. Once it employed three hundred men, who earned about 12½p a day. It extended for a mile into the hill and needed a two-mile long flue, which ran along the ground. It closed in 1888 because of severe flooding and the low price of lead.

Follow the lane to a narrow road, which you cross. Pass through a gate and continue to the railway track. Cross and head to the far right corner to join another road. Turn left and walk on to take a signposted footpath into woodland on your right. After 50 yards turn left and walk through larch to a gate out of the trees. Continue along beside the wall and then at the fence follow it left and right to pass through a waymarked metal gate. Strike across the parkland ahead, steadily descending towards the access track to Bolton Hall, which you join by a gate. Stroll on in the same general direction into the village of Wensley.

Pass the village green on your left, with its pump and a seat just made for a picnic. While in this lovely village visit its glorious church, just below the green and on the road to Middleham. Then walk on along this road to cross a bridge over a fast-running beck. An old mill still has its waterwheel upstream. Take the next lane immediately to the left of the bridge and continue to a waymarked gate on the right. Continue to climb the next stile and then follow the waymarked telephone poles to the next one. Beyond strike uphill to continue on the left of a small wood. Follow the clear track through a succession of stiled fields.

Continue through a gate bearing slightly left to a waymark on a large tree and walk on, keeping to the left of a barn. Go over two more stiles to join Low Wood Lane, where you turn left to walk to the main road, turning right to return to the market place.

ALONG THE WAY:
Holy Trinity Church, Wensley:
Built in 1245 on the site of an ancient Saxon church is one of the most impressive in the dales. Parts of the church were added in the 14th- and 15th-century and the tower in the 18th.

Glorious oak carved stalls in the chancel have poppy heads and carvings of heraldic beasts. On the floor of the sanctuary is a splendid brass which commemorates Sir Simon de Wenslawe, a 14th-century priest. It has a wooden screen and wooden reliquary from Easby Abbey. The reliquary is thought to have contained the remains of St Agatha. There are two 17th-century box pews installed by the third Duke of Bolton. Look for the Jacobean font (1662) and for the standard of the Dales Volunteers raised by Lord Bolton during the Napoleonic Wars. It has many more treasures which youngsters will enjoy finding, and time should be allowed for this on the walk.